Gender on the agenda

Gender on the agenda

Factors motivating boys and girls in MFLs

Ann Clark

For Dave

ACKNOWLEDGEMENTS

I would like to thank all the pupils, their teachers and headteachers in many schools for talking to me about their perceptions of language learning. Their insights have been invaluable.

Thank you also to Mike Calvert and Elaine Millard for helpful comments on an earlier draft.

First published 1998

ISBN 1 902031 19 9

A catalogue record for this book is available from the British Library
Printed in Great Britain by Copyprint UK Ltd

Published by the Centre for Information on Language Teaching and Research, 20 Bedfordbury, Covent Garden, London, WC2N 4LB
Typesetting by Gawcott Typesetting, Milton Keynes MK17 9JP
Cover Design by Marc Padellec

CILT Publications are available from: Grantham Book Services, Isaac Newton Way, Alma Park Industrial Estate, Grantham, Lincs NG31 8SD. Tel: 01476 541 080. Fax: 01476 541 061. Book trade representation (UK and Ireland): Broadcast Book Services, 24 De Montfort Road, London SW16 1LZ. Tel: 0181 677 5129.

Contents

Introduction

The introduction of GCSE in 1988 had a significant impact on the teaching of modern languages, not only widening the appeal of what was traditionally a subject for an elite minority, but also contributing to a gradual increase in the number of pupils studying a modern foreign language to the age of sixteen in advance of the mandatory requirement of a modern foreign language for five years, imposed by the introduction of the National Curriculum. Thus by 1996, the percentages of Y11 pupils taking GCSE in modern languages were as follows: 53% French, 21% German, 6% Spanish, 3% Other Modern Languages (Statistical Bulletin, 1997, DfEE). Table 1 shows the steady rise in the number of pupils taking GCSE French over a number of years expressed as a percentage of sixteen-year old pupils.

	Percentage attempting GCSE			Percentage gaining grade A–C		
	Boys	Girls	Total	Boys	Girls	Total
1988/89	34	49	41	17	26	21
1992/93	48	59	53	19	30	24
1995/96	49	58	53	20	32	26

Table 1: GCSE attempts and achievements in French by fifteen-year old pupils (those in all schools who were fifteen at the start of the academic year).

The table also shows a significant difference in the percentage of boys and girls gaining grades A–C. Thus in 1996, whilst 32% of girls nationally achieved grades A*–C in French, only 20% of boys did so. The disparity in performance between boys and girls at GCSE, which is particularly marked in the language curriculum, has become a very high profile issue with the publication of school league tables. Media coverage has sought to raise awareness about the gender gap and a degree of moral panic has been engendered about failing boys. As the 'standards' debate has widened, so the desperate search for solutions and panaceas has commenced. The Ofsted report (1993) into *Boys and English* noted that the reasons for boys' under performance in English were not easily definable. This is doubtless because it is more than simply a case of gender; the reasons are multi-faceted and complex, involving the influences of parental background, peers and the media, but also the impact of rapid, major social changes in terms of the work force and the nature of traditional family forms.

This book attempts to raise some of the issues in terms of gender and the teaching of modern languages to all for five years, by focusing on pupil and teacher accounts of the language learning process.

1. Pupil perspectives

INTRODUCTION

A CAVEAT

In writing about pupils and gender, I am acutely aware of the problems of considering boys and girls as unitary subjects, when many other factors impinge on their attitudes towards school, as well as on their performance in the classroom and in externally assessed examinations. In this context, variables such as intelligence and socio-economic background play a significant role in pupil performance. Thus amongst high achievers, there is little perceivable difference in attitudes and achievement between boys and girls, whereas with average and below average learners, girls are generally seen to be better motivated and more conscientious. Equally, pupils from professional backgrounds are more accepting across the gender divide of the need to study a modern language. By contrast, pupils from lower socio-economic backgrounds are more likely to be indifferent, if not ethnocentric.

BACKGROUND TO THE RESEARCH

I embarked on a series of pupil and teacher interviews in the early 1990s, with a view to illuminating reasons for boys' comparative under-achievement in modern languages. I interviewed in the region of 250 pupils in gender and ability groups of three or four pupils (able girls, able boys, average girls, average boys, below average girls and below average boys) over a period of 5 years. Additionally, I analysed questionnaires from the whole Year 11 population in 3 schools (396 respondents) about their perceptions of the study of a modern foreign language. (The interview schedules can be found in Appendix 1 and a copy of the questionnaire in Appendix 2). The insights gained from these interviews proved fascinating in terms of boys' and girls' attitudes towards language learning in general, and I will quote from these extensively in this book. They were largely not, however, gender specific. Indeed, as suggested above, intelligence and class seemed to have a much greater influence on pupil perceptions than gender. Boys' under-performance in modern languages is merely symptomatic of their under-achievement in the language curriculum as a whole. The reasons for this are complex, relating partly to the different socialisation of boys and girls from the earliest years, which is further reflected in the gendered nature of the curriculum, and in a differential approach to schooling.

THE GENDERED CURRICULUM AND MODERN LANGUAGES POST–16

Given that pupils (and particularly boys) are no longer allowed to exercise the option to vote with their feet and abandon their study of a foreign language before the end of KS4, the gender stereotyping in the curriculum witnessed previously under the options system has all but disappeared. However, a glance at the statistics for 'A' Level study (see Table 2) immediately demonstrates that at this level there are still very clear notions of gender-appropriate choices.

Subject	Males 16–18	Females 16–18
French	6,859	16,666
English	22,286	55,509
Maths	34,708	20,014
Physics	22,387	6,211

Table 2 shows entries for specific subjects in all schools and colleges in 1995/96 (Source: DfEE Statistical Bulletin, 6/97, HMSO, 1997)

The statistics quoted above show a dramatic gender polarisation post-16, which must inevitably have a backwash effect – as pupils begin to make choices about their future, they doubtless expend their energies accordingly. Despite efforts at an inclusive curriculum for boys and girls and the work of projects such as GIST (Girls into Science and Technology) and WISE (Women into Science and Engineering), girls and boys still continue to make gender-based choices. It could be argued that there are 'hidden agendas' which affect their perception of the subject matter and their consequent ability to do well in it. They may be subconsciously affected by what they deem to be appropriate subject choices, and it may be that they feel the need to act out the feminine/masculine role they sense society expects of them at school. Furthermore, it may be the case that they expend their efforts accordingly so that they do indeed perform best in those subjects which they see as commensurate with their sex.

Some researchers (Macdonald, 1980) have argued that certain school subjects acquire a masculine image and others a feminine one. Once a subject acquires a masculine image, participation in it can be seen to enhance a boy's masculinity and diminish a girl's femininity. It is interesting, however, that research has confirmed that there is a tendency towards a greater polarisation of feelings concerning school subjects in mixed schools (Stables, A., 1990). Moreover, they have noted that an interest in modern languages tends to be greater in single sex than in mixed schools generally. One could attribute this to a variety of reasons – in boys' schools, boys are more likely to have male linguists as role models, they are not overshadowed by girls' superior performance and less likely to feel the need to assert their masculinity in their choice of 'male' subjects.

The statistics do not, however, merely raise questions about the gendered nature of post-16 choices. For modern linguists, it must be a matter of concern that such a small percentage of pupils decide to study a modern foreign language to Advanced Level. It seems to suggest that the subject is unpopular or is perceived to be a difficult option and therefore not in the student's best interests. It is certainly the case that there is a formidable gap, and to some extent a mismatch, between the expectations of the GCSE examination and those of 'A' Level. Ironically, the subject matter at 'A' Level becomes more 'adult', dealing with contemporary issues and concerns, and is therefore of more obvious interest to a young person.

It could well be the case that the review of education for the age range 14–19 will recommend a broadening of the subjects studied post–16. Some would argue that students should be encouraged to learn another foreign language as part of their core curriculum post-16 in line with many of our European counterparts (see Hawkins, E., 1996). It remains to be seen whether the supply of teachers of modern languages makes it possible to even contemplate such a move.

THE IMPACT OF FOREIGN LANGUAGES FOR ALL

The move towards a foreign language for all for five years, brought about by the introduction of the National Curriculum, does not appear to have had the impact one might have hoped on pupil motivation. Pupils' attitudes continue to be influenced by factors such as the relevance of a subject for their future working lives, the comparative difficulty of the subject and the intrinsic interest of the subject matter. On all these counts modern languages prove problematic for many pupils.

RELEVANCE

When pupils consider the importance of learning a foreign language, some are inclined to be dismissive, perceiving potential need solely in terms of either tourist contexts, or along narrow vocational lines. Other core subjects, by contrast, seem to be more readily accepted.

> *'Like Maths, you can see a reason for doing Maths. I know French, like if you go on holiday or if you want to work in France, you need a language, but if you don't want to do anything with it, it seems just like a waste of time.'*

> *'It depends what you want to do, doesn't it. If I wanted to be a translator or something in that kind of field where a language is necessary, or a travel agent or something, I'd say it would be important, but if you wanted to be a PE teacher, then it wouldn't be as important.'*

Typically, pupils quote stereotypical jobs, where they feel the study of a foreign language might be useful such as an air hostess or a travel agent, posts which could arguably be more attractive to girls.

Certain remarks appear to be contingent on the pupils' socio-economic background; pupils with middle class parents are more likely to go on holiday in Europe (see also Vee Harris' Pathfinder '*Fair Enough? Equal opportunities and modern languages*', 1992), or to have contacts with people who travel abroad for business and receive visits from foreign counterparts, thus adding weight to the notion of relevance.

> *'So we've always had German visitors, so, even though I didn't actually speak that much German to them, it probably does help, because it gives me more of an interest.'*

DIFFICULTY

Most pupils commented on the comparative difficulty of the study of a foreign language. This notion

in fact appears to be corroborated by a statement in the DfEE's Statistical Bulletin (1996 & 1997) that –

> *'in the majority of subjects, the most common grade obtained by 15-year old candidates was grade C . . . whereas in French it was D'.*

Memory

In particular, the burden on memory was consistently mentioned by pupils, seen to be difficult and often demotivating –

> *'It's just basically remembering – that's the hard bit'*.

Many felt it was more time-consuming to learn things in a foreign language than in another subject because of the need to learn different 'layers' of meaning, such as the need to remember the word, the gender, the spelling, and the pronunciation. Interestingly, pupils noted that it is more difficult to learn disparate items of vocabulary and grammar than to learn aspects of other subjects which are held together by a narrative thread –

> *'I think with languages I don't actually feel I'm getting anywhere – at the end of the lesson I feel I've learnt another 10–15 words, but it doesn't feel I'm any closer to a goal, whereas with Science I've learnt a new section and it feels like I'm getting somewhere, with languages, it just seems that there is so much I don't know'.*

There are notable differences in attitudes towards learning vocabulary, influenced largely by ability, with able pupils having the capacity to learn vocabulary very quickly, and less able pupils overwhelmed by the sheer volume of vocabulary required.

Concentration

The degree of concentration required in a modern languages lessons was consistently cited as more demanding than in other areas of the curriculum –

> *'You've got to concentrate all the way through it or else you miss a bit, and then later on in the lesson you don't know what's happening'.*

By contrast, in other subjects, pupils reported that they could 'switch off' momentarily and then refocus their attention at a later stage in the lesson without difficulty.

Grammar and self-expression

Able pupils at times expressed frustration at their inability to express themselves because of their lack of knowledge –

'If you want to say something and you can't – so you have to just not put it in or say something else.'

The same pupils, however, as illustrated in the following extract, were positive about learning grammar as they felt this put less burden on their memory, since they could construct sentences themselves rather than having to learn long set phrases without any understanding –

'Dave: *It's good to actually know you're constructing a sentence, know why you're doing it, and know that you've got it right*

Tom: *Because if we're just given phrases to learn then . . .*

Richard: *You don't really see the pattern of it do you?*

Tom: *Yes and it's less easy to remember as well*

Carl: *Yes, that's it, you don't see the pattern*

Dave: *It's easier when, instead of learning phrases, you can think, oh, I know how to say that phrase by constructing it.*

Tom: *You can use your own knowledge rather than your memory.'*

Listening

Many pupils interviewed also expressed a profound dislike for listening, typically commenting that the tapes were 'too fast'. The lack of control over the material inspired panic in many, and their lack of confidence hindered them from tackling even relatively straightforward listening tasks with an open mind.

Private/individual listening

Pupils I have taught at 'A' Level have commented on the difference 'private' listening makes to a task (by this I mean the option to listen to a tape through a personal stereo). In the course of their studies, this gives them more control as they can rewind and listen to a particularly difficult excerpt as many times as they like. They can pause the tape to write notes so as not to place an undue burden on their memory. In short, they can work at their own pace without being distracted or 'phased' by others who appear to know all the answers. In the examination setting, they felt that individual listening helped, as they were less aware of extraneous noise and more able to concentrate.

Individual listening or, alternatively, group listening can be used lower down the school as part of a flexible learning situation, in order to promote more positive attitudes to listening.

Target language

Pupils' views on the target language were essentially polarised. Some were extremely positive, feeling the simulated immersion supported their learning –

'He spoke the whole lesson in German and it does help because you pick up odd words and you remember them, and it helps when you have the constant speaking in German.'

'I think it's a good idea for the teacher to speak the language, because then you are constantly getting it drummed into your head, and you are constantly hearing the words, so you know what they sound like and so on. But if the person is speaking English and writing on the board, you don't actually hear it, you just read it and it doesn't go in.'

Others experienced the use of the target language as very demanding in terms of concentration and comprehension, finding the relentless stream of the foreign language alienating and demotivating.

'They just start talking to you in German without telling you what it is, and they've not taught you and they are rambling on about things you don't understand, so you switch off and you don't listen.'

'She just yabs (sic) on and on – it gets really boring . . . you just get side-tracked and start writing on your pencil case or something.'

These two positions are mirrored in the findings of a recent survey on *Target language use* (Dickson, 1996) and in research carried out in Sweden with teachers of English. In both instances, there was a feeling that the potential for TL use is limited with less able pupils or indeed that it can have a negative effect on pupil attitudes. By contrast, the use of the TL had positive results with more able pupils. Whilst language teachers are united in their support for maximising pupil access to the foreign language, there is perhaps a need for flexibility within the National Curriculum doctrine which allows for a differentiated approach to support pupils' needs appropriately.

TEACHING LEARNER STRATEGIES

It is perhaps salutary to remind ourselves that the skill of listening with this degree of precision and concentration is not required or practised elsewhere in the curriculum, and it is therefore essential that strategies for approaching listening are discussed and practised (see Vee Harris' Pathfinder '*Teaching learners how to learn*', 1997, CILT). Additionally, in order to build pupils' confidence in this skill, it is vital for the teacher to select passages for listening which are not too daunting, or if necessary to adapt either the text or the tasks set, certainly in the initial stages of learning a foreign language, so that pupils can experience success. The same is true of learning vocabulary, which again is an area of the modern languages curriculum which does not receive complementary support elsewhere in the curriculum. It is essential for teachers to discuss with their pupils ways in which they go about learning vocabulary and to suggest other strategies which they might usefully employ. Feelings of success have been shown to be important prerequisites for motivation. In the HMI report (1985) '*Boys and modern languages*', two of the major reasons given for boys opting to continue with their studies of a modern language, were if they had enjoyed the subject and experienced success. It is a matter of concern that in some cases the initial enthusiasm for a 'new' subject at the beginning of KS3 can so rapidly wane and dissipate.

'My French teacher said I won't do very well, so I thought why bother with that when I can spend an extra ten minutes on another subject that I know I'm going to do well in and I could just pick up another grade.'

'I'd love to think that I could go to another country and talk their language and stuff like that but you don't feel you are achieving anything. In Science you think – "Oh yeah, I understand that, I've worked that out" or "Oh yeah, I know how to do that bit" but in French there's none of that. You don't feel like you're getting anywhere.'

Failure in the early stages of language learning can make five years of language learning and teaching seemingly interminable for all parties concerned! One of the key challenges therefore, is how teachers can make the tedium and sheer hard work of learning both more approachable and more palatable.

INTRINSIC INTEREST OR *'I THINK FRENCH IS A BIT OF A DRAG'*

Whilst the transactional emphasis of the GCSE examination represents an enormous step forward when compared with the artificiality of the 'O' Level syllabi, it is nonetheless a middle class syllabus based on the notion of families holidaying in Europe, staying in hotels and eating in restaurants. For pupils from lower socio-economic backgrounds, these contexts doubtless seem equally artificial, or as remote as some of the subjects selected for translation in the 'O' Level examinations. Furthermore, although the GCSE claims to be a 'communicative' syllabus, the format of the examination has often been very prescriptive, essentially requiring translation both in the role play situations and in many of the writing tasks.

Many pupils interviewed commented on the irrelevance of the subject matter in modern languages for them. It could well be true, as Powell (1986) suggested, that pupils find much of the material and its transactional 'tourist situation' context anodyne. Indeed, it could be the case that at an age where personal image is important, when pupils are searching for a voice to express themselves, they find much of the subject matter dull, superficial and irrelevant.

'Some of the stuff we've learnt is kind of pointless, because I mean some of the conversations that we have it's not the kind of thing that you'd have in conversation with a French person '

In interviews, pupils who had been abroad commented on the gaps in their knowledge which meant that they could ask someone to pass the salt but did not know the word for boyfriend and could not ask if they could stay at a friend's house!

Many pupils also commented on the repetitive nature of their language learning (*'we do the same things every lesson, over and over again'*). Certain topics had obviously been covered several times in the course of five years' study and consequently lost any appeal they might initially have had *'It just gets so boring after five years, and like now you just can't be bothered.'* The justification for their learning and their own motivation had both dissipated and they were left with a sense of endlessly rehearsing with no performance in sight.

Given these comments, it is important to think not only of the subject matter included in departmental schemes of work, but also of the treatment of topics. Many pupils have responded very positively to moves towards greater creativity and the opportunity this allows for making a more personally relevant statement. Motivation seems to stem from pupils sensing that the language activities correspond to what they feel they need to learn.

Gendered attitudes towards work

It has been argued that pupils' experience of the same teacher in the same room is different. Boys' monopoly of physical and linguistic space and teacher attention has been well documented (Scott, Spender, Stanworth, Mahoney). In her observation of English 'A' Level classes, where there were more girls than boys, Stanworth (1983) noted that for every four boys who participated in classroom discussion, there was one girl; for every two boys who asked a question, there was one girl. In random classroom observations conducted by an advisory teacher in connection with research I was previously involved in (Clark & Trafford, 1994), it was noted that in a class with almost twice as many girls (seven boys and twelve girls), the boys had 36 interactions with the teacher (of which fifteen were initiated by the boys) whilst the girls had only 22 interactions with the teacher (only one of which was initiated by a girl). Significantly, it was the teacher's intention to be even-handed and he was not aware of the extent to which his attention favoured the boys. This scenario has been shown to be fairly typical in classrooms.

Both teachers and pupils themselves acknowledge that girls generally are much more conscientious and boys more likely to *'muck around'*, *'doss'*, talk, show off in class and *'have a laugh'*. It is considered 'normal' for boys to shout out, jostle one another, engage in 'play fighting'. Boys are reprimanded in school more often than girls. It has been estimated that the ratio of praise to blame is as low as 1:3 for boys. Although attention is drawn to boys' bad behaviour, many teachers find boys' irreverent attitudes attractive. Teachers across the curriculum have often pandered to the boys in the interests of retaining classroom control, given that girls are typically more malleable, more tolerant of boring tasks and more concerned to please and 'do the right thing' (Kelly, 1987). Girls are often better at planning and organising their work, but they may also work harder as they lack confidence in their own ability. Boys are greater risk-takers, whereas girls are typically low profile, not risking getting an answer wrong in class. Girls who do not choose to mimic the stereotype of the retiring female, may face considerable antagonism from their peers. Being intelligent, asking or indeed answering questions in class may expose both boys and girls to accusations of being a 'swot' or 'boffin'. Thus many pupils have to tread an uneasy path if they want to be accepted.

Homework

Girls seem generally to be much more conscientious about doing homework. Other researchers (Harris et al., 1993) found that whereas many girls in KS4 worked two or three hours an evening as well as at the weekend, boys claimed to do up to three hours per week. This is doubtless attributable to a large extent to the differential expectations for boys and girls. Outside school, boys appear to have more freedom and more of a social life and consequently to devote less time to homework. However, boys are also subject to a considerable amount of peer pressure; they want to subscribe to the dominant sub-culture, to be considered not as a 'swot' but instead as 'one of the lads'. Askew and Ross (1988) quoting from a 14-year old in a mixed London comprehensive school express the tension felt particularly by boys –

'It's hard if you want to get on in school because you're expected to participate in the messing around, especially if you're a boy.'

Other researchers including Delamont (1990) have remarked on the importance of friendship groups among boys in school –

Membership of and adherence to the norms and values of a particular peer group can make a difference to the school attainment and involvement of the boys. A boy whose friends work hard and share the teachers' values is likely to work hard and be tuned in to the teacher's values himself.'

It may be true that boys claim to spend so little time on personal study because doing homework is not 'cool'. Clearly, in many cases, school ranks lower down in boys' priorities and they feel the need to demonstrate their masculinity through resistance to school. Where girls are resistant to school, they tend to demonstrate it in more subtle ways (possibly by flouting the school uniform policy, wearing too much jewellery or make-up) rather than in direct confrontational terms.

Relationship with the teacher

The pupil interviews revealed that the rapport with the member of staff teaching them had a profound effect on their attitudes and motivation. Where the relationship was good, pupils were more positive about the subject.

'You take a lot more in, because they make it a lot more fun to be there, you know, you'd rather be there than you would a different lesson, because it depends on the teacher and what the teacher's like really, and how well you get on with them.'

Although a high proportion of language teachers are women, the gender of the member of staff was considered unimportant compared with the teacher/pupil relationship. When asked what pupils thought to be the qualities of a good language teacher, they suggested that teachers should know their subject and explain things well, be a good listener, make learning fun so pupils can remember things better, be helpful, patient, friendly and approachable, enthusiastic and encouraging, strict but fair, have a sense of humour and be understanding! Above all, they wanted a teacher who –

'realises not everyone is born to speak French'.

Pupils also seemed to value a productive dialogue with a teacher and the notion of a learning partnership. Some schools are currently building in time at KS4 for teachers and pupils to consult and review their progress, discussing areas of weakness and ways in which these might be addressed. Such a policy encourages pupils to take stock, and gives them the opportunity to take responsibility for their learning. A possible pro-forma to inform this teacher/pupil dialogue can be found in Appendix 3.

Making languages more enjoyable: possible strategies

There was a very strong feeling that enjoyment was linked to success and that therefore, if a pupil was good at a subject, she or he was more likely to enjoy it.

> *'I think it's a circle – if you're no good at it, you're not going to enjoy it'.*

- Pupils thought variety was important. They welcomed variety in the learning styles offered. Several felt that more use could be made of a range of media such as radio, television, IT. *'You could watch five minutes from a TV programme like Eastenders in French.'*

- Pupils seemed interested to know more about the culture and customs of the foreign countries.

- More use of games *'it makes it more interesting and more enjoyable, and like people want to participate more instead of just messing about, because it's something that they enjoy doing'.*

- More role play and integration of drama – *'we used to make our own role plays on the subject we'd just been covering. We used to get a group together and sort it out – we used to mess around, but we did it and it was a good laugh. Then we'd do it in front of the class . . . Practical work in French is important because you can't remember anything by just writing it down. I think when you are doing practical stuff you remember things better.'*

- More opportunity to visit the foreign country. Pupils who had visited the foreign country were positive about the experience. *'I learnt a lot from going to France and I found it really enjoyable'.* One boy interviewed regretted the fact that he had not been able to try out his French – *'It's good to put into practice what you've learnt, you know, then you feel satisfied, I mean now we've learnt all this but we haven't put it into practice because we haven't been to France or anything.'* Short study visits in the early years of language learning, perhaps as part of an activities week, help to give pupils a flavour of the country and to contextualise their learning.

- Alternatives to school exchanges and the classic school trip (which may appeal more to girls), such as combining a trip to France with outward bound type activities involving the games department as well as the modern languages department, or work experience in France/Germany/Spain for pupils in KS4 and beyond.

- Contact with native speakers *'I think having somebody from France to come in like and talk to us'.* Pupils spoke positively about foreign language assistants (FLAs) *'I think we should have more time to speak to the French Assistant, because it's different when you're speaking to your teacher and when you're speaking to a French person'.* In schools where there were FLAs, but students did not have any contact with them because this was restricted to the 'A' level students or the top sets, several pupils regretted this. Not only are FLAs younger and therefore arguably more likely to be familiar with or share some of the aspects of the youth culture of the young people in school, they are powerful role models of young people who are motivated to learn a foreign language and who can remember and therefore empathise with the difficulties some of the pupils experience.

- Opportunities offered by new technology such as e-mail links or video-conferencing to allow young people to communicate directly with their counterparts in Europe on subjects of interest to them. Such links provide a real audience for the otherwise pointless penfriend letters and allow for quick responses, in contrast to the more familiar and protracted penfriend letter exchanges.

- More group work. Several respondents reported on the fact that they found it helpful to work in groups, learning from and supporting one another. *'I like group work best, you can work together and you get to learn the vocabulary a lot quicker that way.' 'It's helpful when you have someone else, because sometimes the thing you know, they don't know and vice versa.'*

- More help with learning strategies – *'if they can try and think of ways of making you remember things – they can say this is an important word, you've got to remember it. I remember it by thinking of 'X' or by linking it to this . . . '* and with revision – *'sometimes when it comes to revision, we don't have a lot of work to revise from, because when we are listening to tapes then we'll just write one word answers in English, and it's a bit difficult to revise because we haven't got sentences and we haven't got a lot of grammar to revise from.'*

2. Teacher perspectives

Introduction

In the course of teacher interviews, a cross-section of teachers of different languages and different amounts of experience offered their insights into the differential performance of boys and girls. Teachers were asked to comment on pupils' perceptions of modern languages; which aspects of the course pupils enjoyed and which they disliked. Further, I asked if they were aware of gender differences in terms of attitudes, approach to work in class and at home, learning styles and achievement. Finally, I enquired about grouping for teaching.

In this chapter, I have tried to let experienced practitioners speak for themselves, quoting directly so that teachers can compare their own views with those articulated here.

Teachers on the record

The promotion of foreign languages outside school

> *'Languages are seen as a significantly low priority by too many people in the UK . . . I think the higher profile activities and the promotion of languages has to be emphasised outside school as well as inside school. We are looking for UK role models to give examples to pupils of the value of being able to use a foreign language not only in their work environment, but in a social and cultural environment.'*

Parental expectations – 'they all speak English'

'Increasing recognition of English as the world vehicle language also encourages a short-sighted acceptance of monolingualism. Sadly, even universities, of all places, have seemed to encourage this complacency. And, among employers, complacency dies hard' (Hawkins, 1996:18). The continuing dominance enjoyed by English, spoken in the UK, widely in North America and Australasia, through the language of pop culture and Information Technology (notably the Internet) does little to convince many pupils or parents of the need for pupils in this country to study a foreign language.

> *'I think as English people, our expectations have been that foreign languages don't count. It was always a very elitist subject when the majority of us – even our parents were taught at school, and there was this feeling that I was no good at French or German, I was no good at any foreign language, and therefore I don't expect my children to be.'*

Given that many parents did not themselves study a modern language to examination level at sixteen, there is a pressing need to communicate with them and to enlist their support. The best arena for this

might be at a new intake evening, where information could be given about the course their children are likely to follow in modern languages. Additionally, it would be useful to suggest to them ways in which they can become involved (some may choose to learn alongside their children) and help their children (for example by helping them to learn vocabulary). It is important for pupil motivation that their parents value the subject –

> *'Supportive parental attitudes will quite often generate positive attitudes among pupils'.*

The gendered curriculum

> *'It does seem that girls are more amenable to studying foreign languages. They don't regard it as being, in any way out of place for them to do well, to study to the best of their ability. Whereas boys, for some unidentifiable sort of reason, in the majority don't seem to see it as the norm for a boy to do well to study modern languages.'*

Hawkins criticises the introduction of a foreign language at age eleven (Year 7), suggesting that this is particularly difficult for boys: *'We choose to introduce it just at the onset of adolescence, when "empathy", the capacity to share another's feelings, which is so strong in 7/8 year olds, gives way to self-consciousness and insecurity. This is especially true of boys. We challenge them to "go to meet" an unfamiliar language and culture, just when they feel least secure in their own.'* (1996:17)

Maturity

> *'I find it particularly striking here that the girls, when they come in at Year 7, seem so much more mature, generally, than the boys. And they respond to the pressures of work and concentration, and they seem to get stuck into things more than the boys; you have a lot of silliness from the boys. That then creates . . . tension between the teacher and the pupils. In turn that results in a lack of achievement, and then by the time they get to the end of Year 8, that builds up and they haven't got the maturity to see that they should be working and so on. And then you go into setting and of course they're not achieving so they go into a lower set.'*

Although the study of a new language theoretically presents pupils with a tabula rasa at the age of eleven, in practice girls generally have more highly developed language skills (as witnessed by their superior performance in English at seven and eleven), and are consequently better equipped to deal with the demands of studying a new language. It is therefore hardly surprising to find a preponderance of girls in top sets after the first year.

Presentation skills

> *'Girls generally will take more care over written work . . . It will look actually seductively better to the teacher marking at a first glance . . . on further investigations, you know, quite often the boys' work is worth much more than it looks at first sight.'*

'I think that because writing takes more time and care, and I think girls tend to . . . , take more time and care over their written work, I think that their written work is better than that of a lot of the boys.'

In many cases, there seems to be a tacit acceptance that boys' work is poorly presented and that this is a natural phenomenon. If we want boys to take more time and care over their written work, teachers across the curriculum need to take a much firmer line on this point. The availability of word processing can motivate boys to devote more time and care to their written work. (See Chapter 3 for a more detailed discussion of ICT).

Attitudes towards work

'I always feel the boys are under-functioning. I never feel they are overdoing it, even if I have a good group. I never feel that they're working to their full potential . . . I think boys of themselves are much more laid back than girls.'

'There's a type of boy in this school, who is very sport-oriented. He's not a, you know, a hooligan or a drop out particularly or antipathetical towards school, but he's very sport orientated. I think the Americans call it "gung-ho" – he wants to be one of the lads. Work, school work, features relatively lower down on his list of importances, and he will rush the work, do the required minimum, in his perception, get it done to his satisfaction and then out of the way and get on with something more important as he sees it.'

'Thinking about the Spanish group. . . I think it's true to say that with the exception of one boy, the better results will be gained by the girls. The one boy will achieve probably a good result and will do so almost entirely on his natural ability. It won't be as a result of working hard. He could have achieved more in fact he is simply coasting – he's got a lot of ability.'

'I think girls come to terms much more with the idea – I might not like this particularly, but at the end of two years I want a decent grade, and I'm going to buckle down and I'm going to get on with it and do it . . . Lads I think, have a much less mature attitude towards things generally, and it's all a bit ad hoc . . . '

Homework

'The girls tended to do homework more frequently than the boys . . . (who) tend to have a fuller social life. They tend to have more things to do. And perhaps be allowed to stop out later, allowed more freedom. That possibly might influence it. I think in general the boys seem to pay less attention to detail.'

'I think the girls perform better with learning homeworks than the boys do. The boys . . . seem to rely on native wit just to get through in my experience.'

'If the learning homework is tested by oral competence in class, then a group of boys will be likely to perform as satisfactorily as a group of girls. If it is tested by written performance, then I would suggest that girls are more likely to perform well than boys.'

A recent publication *'The gender divide: performance differences between boys and girls at school'*, published jointly by Ofsted and the Equal Opportunities Commission reinforced these impressions, noting that girls and boys have different approaches to planning and organising their work. *'Girls are more likely to remember to bring the right equipment to lessons and to complete their homework diaries. They are more likely to respond to teachers' comments on their work.'* They do however comment that these differences become less obvious among high achieving pupils.

There is a case for providing support for homework in school. A classroom set aside twice a week with a member of staff available to help with any queries or problems provides an opportunity to complete homework within the school day and to free up the evening for socialising or other leisure pursuits. Further, some pupils who found languages difficult, commented that they had no one at home to help them with their homework in languages. One boy contrasted his experience with that of Maths, a subject in which he also struggled, but where his father could help him. By contrast, neither parent had studied German, and he remarked that on occasions he could not even start the homework, as he did not understand what he had to do.

'It isn't cool to do well at school'

'I think the males are the shrinking violets. They don't want to participate in something and derive failure out of it and therefore lose face.'

Boys often find it harder to cope with failure than girls, and are more ready to opt out of things they find difficult. Given that all pupils claim to find modern languages difficult, it is important to set short-term achievable goals. The graded test movement did much to motivate average and below average groups, by taking a narrow focus such as a topic area, setting short, accessible tasks in discrete skill areas and allowing pupils to 'retake' if they did not achieve the required pass mark. The provision of school certificates, which some chose to present in assembly, or letters home to parents, were another source of motivation. For average and below average boys, however, the notion of success is itself problematic because of the prevailing 'anti-school' ethos –

'Girls respond to positive encouragement (whereas) the boys would see this as 'sucking up' to the teacher. They do their work in an overtly begrudging way. Otherwise I think they might perhaps lose a little bit of face if they appeared to want to please the teacher.'

There is a real need for a whole school policy to foster a culture of study and learning and to find ways in which boys can achieve without facing the derision of their peers. This is an issue in which parents can also usefully be involved to reinforce the school's message about achievement. Several schools have arranged information evenings with parents to make them aware of the differential achievement between boys and girls in public examinations, and to suggest ways in which they can work together with the school to support their children's learning.

Ironically, although attention is often drawn to boys' bad behaviour, many teachers find boys' irreverent attitudes attractive and may therefore unwittingly encourage their 'off task' behaviour.

Adolescent boys and de-motivation

'Come Year 9, they are getting that bit switched off, they've perhaps plateaud a bit; to actually motivate them and pick them up again – it's asking a lot of the teachers without more resources.'

'Essentially languages is a communicative subject, and you are talking and expressing things, and I think there are very few fourteen, fifteen year old boys in England who are very good at expressing themselves . . . If you were the sort of lad who would do it in English and do it very eloquently, then when they are trying to do it in a foreign language, where they are stumbling and hesitating, I think that makes them feel extremely embarrassed and extremely put off, and sometimes their reaction is to back out of it . . . Lads at that age are much more into doing things with their hands and doing things with machines rather than interacting with people very much.'

Learning styles

'I think in Year 7 there's a very positive attitude that does get less as you go up the school. Because I think it's taught in a very different way from a lot of the other subjects, it's much more teacher centred and I think sometimes it's a bit of a shock for them.'

HMI (1985) found that boys are intolerant of dull and excessively formal teaching. It may be the case that in many classrooms, the majority of the time is spent working together as a whole class which could have implications for pupils' concentration span.

'Boys rush tasks, want to finish, move on, etc.'

'I think the lads need to get on, they can't sort of sit still and I think lads get very restless and turned off by it (MFL), they need a lot of cajoling . . . they need that sort of more rumbustious pace and loads of things to do. The girls tend to be more placid. If you can actually harness the energy of the boys, if it can be channelled into role plays, that actual energy, then I think they can carry on having a positive attitude.'

A.C. Are there any other learning styles that suit boys or girls in particular?

'I think sometimes drama and role play. I noticed when I first came here, I had a Year 8 group and they were very difficult to handle. But whenever I gave them the opportunity to do role play and get clothes and acting out, there were some boys who didn't really achieve an awful lot generally, who really enjoyed it, got into it, and were obviously very good at drama. And I have noticed with some boys that they like to be up and

doing. And active. Rather than just sitting and listening, and often a lot of listening is demanded.'

'I think that they (pupils) *tend to associate using the computers with fun and games.'*

Some teachers commented that girls seemed to concentrate better and for longer than boys. Boys were described as more easily distracted, having lower boredom thresholds, and responding to short, sharp activities with immediate feedback. Girls were considered more tolerant of uninteresting work than boys.

Researchers have found that certain boys may respond better to a tactile or kinaesthetic approach to learning (that is by handling and doing, and through involvement with concrete experiences which have direct application to their own life). Boys' learning styles are often based on trial and error – boys generally have more self-confidence than girls, and are more willing to take risks. By contrast, girls are more reflective, tending to think things through and then respond. Both the language curriculum and the accompanying learning styles may in fact serve to accentuate the differences between girls and boys by favouring the girls' preferred learning styles. It is important to cater for different preferred learning styles by adopting an eclectic approach which will embrace both formal teaching and active/experiential learning.

Relationship with the teacher

'I think the person teaching them is a very important person, and that they tend to identify the subject area with the person who's teaching them. And if the person who's teaching them is an effective teacher, then I think the attitude towards the subject tends to be very positive. And I think the reverse is true as well. I don't think gender comes into it at all. I think it's to do with the effectiveness of the teacher. It demands so much concentration and effort and at some point they have to sit down and learn, so there has to be an inner determination from pupils to want to learn and to make efforts. And there is a greater dependency on the teacher to build up confidence, and showing them that they can do it and they can make progress. And if you don't get the relationship right, and build up the confidence, and that goes, then the pupils can switch off. And once that switching off has started and set in, then it's very difficult to pull them back.'

The impact of work experience

One teacher commented on the value of running work experience visits in a foreign country. She had worked with the PSE and Careers Departments in her school in the planning and organisation of the visit, but felt there was scope for much more cross-curricular development.

'. . . comments they (pupils) made in their report about how well foreigners speak English. It brought that home to them much more than I can, however often I say it in class. It was a real motivator – and the fact that they felt they had improved particularly in their comprehension, all of them; even the weakest – and they had gained so much in confidence in all sorts of ways, not just on the language front.'

IMPROVING THE MOTIVATION OF BOYS

'They've got to feel they're achieving, and therefore you've got to organise your tasks and organise your work to make sure they do achieve.'

WHAT ABOUT THE GIRLS?

'One of the things that has distressed me (. . .) is that KS4 girls are so low in self-esteem, and their sights are so low. Girls who are going to get 6 or 7 grade 'A's at GCSE will say "I want to be a hairdresser, because I'm not really much good for anything else" – there's nothing wrong with being a hairdresser – it's their perceptions and their aspirations are far, far too low.'

STAFFING

'I'd like to redress it (the imbalance between male and female staff in the department – nine female and one male). It is important, because even if pupils don't see, don't make any obvious statement about it affecting them, I think it does, it says something very clearly about role models. I'm sure again it's subconscious, but although I still go back to the point about the relationship with the teacher and pupil being central, I still think it would be nice to have more men within the department. I think anyway, men and women generally look at life from different perspectives. And therefore I think working as a team, you might – with more men around – have a slightly different perspective on certain things, certain issues. And I think the broader perspective you can get in any debate is better.' (female HOD)

'I think I would be happier if there were more male teachers in the faculty . . . I think as a subject we need to have a better balance of role models for the pupils to respond to.' (male HOD)

Hawkins' (1996) suggests that the disproportion of male and female staff teaching modern languages is unlikely to change:

'That the male/female teaching imbalance in language classrooms throughout the UK is set to intensify is suggested by the figures of graduates applying to train as teachers:

The effect of role models on pupils' career choices has obvious implications for the position of languages post–16, recruitment for university and future supply of teachers.' (pp7–8)

It remains a vexed question to what extent the sex of the teacher can have an influence on pupils' perception of a particular subject area. Whilst pupils tend to deny that the sex of their language teacher affects them, it seems likely that this communicates certain messages about gender-appropriate subjects, in the same way as principally male science or CDT departments convey a subliminal message about their subjects.

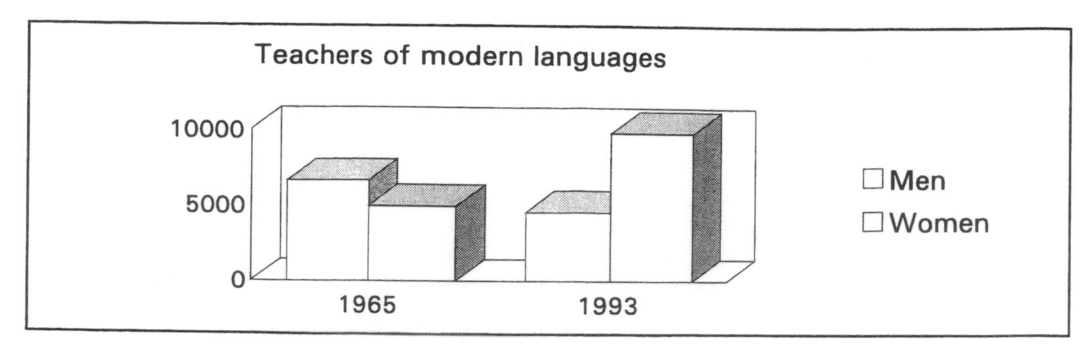

RESOURCING AND TIMETABLING

'I think it would be easier for me to inspire people if I wasn't teaching in English rooms, Maths rooms or whatever else rooms.'

'We still only get 2 hours a week. I don't think it's really enough.'

Resourcing and timetabling are two contentious, arguably insoluble problems. Given that modern languages is the only compulsory subject which is new to pupils in KS3, there does seem to be a strong argument for allocating it more curriculum time. There are, however, so many conflicting demands on the timetable that non-linguists do not share this view. The issue of resourcing is another valid point. One of the key findings from pupil interviews and questionnaires was that pupils like variety both of presentation and of tasks. Clearly, teaching in a series of non-language rooms far away from available resources militates against this.

CONCLUSIONS

Teachers interviewed covered a wide range of issues. At times the issues are beyond the scope of the individual modern languages department. Some of the insights gained can, however, help to illuminate the different ways of working of boys and girls, and help to inform future planning and practice.

A DEPARTMENTAL AUDIT

Staff might find it helpful to look at the status quo in their school before discussing the impact of gender on their department. The following questions are intended as an aide-memoire – it is recognised that not all questions will apply to all schools.

- What proportion of boys and girls gain grades A*– C at GCSE in modern languages?
- How does this compare with their performance in other areas of the curriculum (for example, English, Mathematics)?

- What proportion of boys and girls are in which sets? Is there a predominance of girls in the top set and boys in the bottom set?

- What proportion of boys and girls opt to continue studying a FL beyond GCSE?

- What proportion of boys and girls are involved in (a) school exchanges (b) language department trips?

Notes for departmental discussion

Appendix 4 is designed as a potential starting point for departmental discussions on issues of gender and modern languages. Teachers could complete the grid individually and then compare their responses with colleagues, discussing the major concerns which emerge for their individual department.

It is hoped that the following questions might also provide a useful framework for departmental discussion.

- How does our current setting policy affect boys' and girls' perceptions of their aptitude for modern languages?

- Do the learning styles we use most frequently favour certain 'types' of pupil – whether male/female or academic/non-academic or confident/less confident?

- To what extent do our schemes of work allow for variety and progression between KS3 and KS4?

- Is it true that there is a mismatch between our schemes of work and pupils' maturity and interests at KS4?

- Is the modern languages curriculum intrinsically more appealing to girls? What can we do to make it more boy friendly?

- Given the motivational nature of ICT, how can we maximise our access to IT hardware?

- Can we incorporate ICT tasks into our Schemes of work as core elements of each module of work?

- Can we plan to incorporate relevant video material into the scheme of work?

- What steps can we take to convince pupils of the need and relevance of the study of a modern foreign language?

- Can we present boys with positive role models of men using languages in their work?

- Can we set short-term achievable goals to build in and guarantee success in an effort to improve pupils' self esteem and motivation?

- Can we develop a merit system to reward good written work / good participation orally? (Well done stickers in the foreign language?)
- Can we review our homework policy firstly to ensure that pupils get an appropriate amount of homework, and secondly to devise ways of enabling all pupils to be able to attempt the work?
- Can we review our policy on learning homeworks to raise the profile of learning vocabulary?
- Can we communicate with and involve parents more, enabling them to support their children in various ways?

3. Strategies

Introduction

The drive to raise standards has led to an increasing preoccupation with examination statistics and has brought boys' under-achievement at GCSE to the fore. The corollary to this has been the quest for solutions or panaceas. As I have tried to show, the underlying causes for the current disparity in performance between boys and girls are wide-ranging. In many cases, gendered differences have been learnt through early socialisation. These differences may not have been challenged in school, as teachers may feel that they are inherent rather than learnt. Individual attempts to change the status quo may seem like clutching at straws; what is needed is a whole school policy to redress the inequities and inconsistencies in the treatment of boys and girls. Such a whole school policy will inevitably embrace a variety of strategies, some of which are discussed below.

Grouping for teaching

All ability groupings

Some schools have experimented with a variety of setting procedures in an attempt to improve the motivation and performance of boys in modern languages. The familiar pattern produced by a policy of setting by ability, typically leads to a preponderance of girls and a tiny minority of boys in the top sets. By contrast, bottom sets tend to be full of demotivated and often disaffected boys. The covert message seems to be that languages is a subject for the girls and the 'boffins', although, in interviews, if asked whether modern languages was a boys' or girls' subject, pupils felt it was a subject for both.

The disparity in numbers in the different sets has inspired certain schools to adopt mixed or all ability groupings in KS3, and some to continue with this policy to the age of sixteen, in the hope of maintaining a positive attitude towards the subject across the gender and ability divide. In addition, some feel that this policy allows boys the opportunity to mature later than the girls, and not be 'written off' by premature setting arrangements which are potentially self-fulfilling. As with any policy, however, this approach inevitably has drawbacks. Whilst it may help to maintain good order and foster a positive working atmosphere in the classroom, avoiding the nightmare of the notorious 'sink set', it may also, as Ofsted (1994) have suggested, have a detrimental effect on pupil performance –

> *'the pupils' achievement in all years beyond Year 7 was usually higher in setted groups than in mixed ability groups.'*

Moys (1996) proposes another alternative to redress the gender imbalance caused by setting by 'ability' in the early years, whereby, for example, a set could contain the top fifteen boys and the top fifteen girls rather than the top thirty pupils. Yet another option is to set boys and girls separately in the early years to avoid any disadvantage caused to boys by their later maturation.

Single sex setting

Some schools have (controversially) decided to set pupils according to sex either across the whole curriculum, or simply in certain areas of the curriculum which are felt to be particularly gendered. Such a policy avoids the virtual exclusion of boys from the 'top' sets in subjects such as modern languages and English. Schools tend to create two parallel sets, one for boys and the other for girls. Inevitably, this approach makes the spread of ability in the sets wider, demanding a higher degree of differentiation than in a more rigidly setted situation, but arguably also raising the motivation stakes by offering an improved self image to a greater number of pupils.

One of the benefits of this approach has been to enable staff to target their lesson content more to the needs of individual groups. Some teachers report working to improve boys' presentation in Year 8, offering short term rewards such as merits for neat work. Others report working on study skills and establishing lunch time homework clubs to offer support to those who would not necessarily find it at home, freeing up the evenings when many boys have out of school commitments or meet up with friends, and are therefore more likely to rush their homework or complete it in a minimalist way (if at all). It has been recognised by researchers that the pressure on boys to socialise is infinitely greater than that on girls. Indeed, parents in general are much more protective of girls, who consequently have much less freedom to socialise outside the home in the evenings, and can therefore devote much more time to homework.

Studies on single sex schooling

The recent report (Smithers & Robinson, 1995) '*Co-educational and single-sex schooling*' concludes that single sex grouping may advantage girls, whereas boys are disadvantaged because they miss out on the 'civilising' input of the girls:

> '*. . . there is no suggestion that boys' examination performance is improved by separating the sexes. What evidence there is, tends to suggest that boys can benefit from co-education. There is no doubt, however, that some parents fear that boys could have a dominating and disruptive effect on their daughters' education.*'

Dame Warnock took a similar view and made a strong plea for more girls' schools within the state sector, to enable girls to experience real equality of opportunity and to fulfil their potential –

> '*. . . girls are subject to huge pressures from society. In a single-sex school there is a kind of refuge from that. Girls flourish and make better decisions about their future – they're not afraid to be clever. In mixed schools there is a danger, especially for the less able ones, that they will take on a more conventional role.' (TES, March 1991.)*

Kruse has worked in Denmark researching the possibility of single-sex settings within co-educational schools. She records her observations of a school where fourteen/fifteen year old girls and boys from Grethe Biil's class were segregated for four lessons a week (1996). Biil reported the following differences:

The girls only setting

1. *The girls work in a concentrated way. The subject matter is worked through in half the time used by the boys.*
2. *The girls are well-prepared.*
3. *The girls keep strictly to the subject.*
4. *The girls see the lesson as a shared venture.*
5. *The girls listen and show respect when others speak. They laugh in a caring way: 'Aren't we having a nice time together?'*
6. *The girls are helpful to each other.*

The boys-only setting

1. *The boys are active in an anarchistic way.*
2. *The boys have a low degree of preparation.*
3. *The boys broaden the subject and include new angles and points of view.*
4. *They see the lesson as an individual matter.*
5. *The boys constantly interrupt each other with funny or ironical remarks. They are tough with each other, use swear words and garbage (sic) language.*
6. *The boys compete with each other in getting the teacher's attention..*

Kruse concludes that the different attitudes manifested by the boys and girls forced Biil to adapt her teaching style, first spontaneously, but subsequently deliberately developing different teaching strategies and setting distinct goals for the two groups.

The current climate of concern about boys' under-achievement can, at times, serve to mask the problems experienced by girls who, despite increased awareness of equal opportunities issues, still do not receive an equitable amount of teacher time and attention and may be seen by some teachers as 'colourless' by comparison with the livelier boys. Ironically, girls are currently outperforming their male counterparts regardless of the patterns of interaction in the classroom which tend to favour the boys. Further, the issue of boys' under-achievement indirectly affects the girls, whose progress can be hampered if the teacher routinely has to spend a disproportionate amount of lesson time in managing reluctant or disruptive boys.

PUPIL PERSPECTIVES

SINGLE SEX SETTING: THE ALL GIRLS' GROUPS

When pupils, in one of the sample schools where this experiment had been trialled, were interviewed, there seemed to be a strong sense of the girls feeling more comfortable in a single sex environment, feeling more able to be 'themselves' and not having to put on a show for the boys –

> *'Well I enjoy it much more actually just with girls. I don't know why, because it just seems because you're all the same, and then you don't have to – let's say – impress the boys.'*

> *'I learn more because I just listen more when the boys aren't there.'*

Others mentioned not being afraid of ridicule when they got something wrong, or derision if they got it right and were deemed to be 'a swot'.

> *G: I can talk more in class because I don't get embarrassed if I say something wrong.'*
> *AC: Why do you get embarrassed when the boys are there?*
> *G: Because they laugh at you'.*

Girls commented on the boys' tendency to mess about, cheat at games, 'show off' and generally be disruptive.

> *'It's quite frustrating, because you can't learn anything, because they're always messing around and if ever you try to have a game they always cheat at it.'*

> *'Boys are just more talkative and stuff and if you try to concentrate they're going to think you're stupid or something'.*

Some of the girls who had been taught in a mixed set wished they had had the opportunity to be taught in a single sex set –

> *'I think I would have preferred to have been in an all girls' group. I think you would learn more because the boys in our group aren't too bad, but a lot of boys in other classes shout and mess around quite a lot . . . some of them show off a little bit. They just can't be sensible in a lot of things.'*

In some cases, there was a feeling that the boys were a source of entertainment and amusement because of their tendency to fool around. Some girls thought that teachers made lessons more fun in a mixed situation because this was essential to retain the boys' interest, but in an all girls' group could 'get away with' more academic work.

SINGLE SEX SETTING: THE ALL BOYS' GROUPS

Most boys preferred the mixed environment. Some admitted that they were more likely to show off and mess about when they had an audience (i.e. the girls). Others welcomed the girls' presence because it gave them the opportunity to get on with their work. Boys thought that boys messed around more than girls because '*they want to make people laugh.*' When asked how teachers could get boys to work harder, the two suggestions were that they should be stricter and have work '*that's not boring but fun – like playing games and plays.*'

Some of the boys, however, reported that they liked being taught in an all boys' setting as they felt less inhibited in role plays. Many wished to return to a mixed sex setting arrangement as they thought they benefited from the different ideas and perspectives that girls had to offer. Boys who had been taught in a mixed set did not like the notion of an all boys' set –

> *'It would be really frustrating for the people who want to work hard because there are people messing around.'*

Teacher perspectives

Single sex setting

Whilst some staff were cautious about 'experimenting' with pupils' education, they were generally positive about the single sex experiment. One member of staff working with the top set all girls' group commented on the 'work-orientated atmosphere', noting that she was able to go into work in more depth and also that the quieter girls were more willing to volunteer answers in an all girls' set.

> *'I think it's benefited the quieter ones and sometimes the more able ones and also those that are a bit nervous about speaking up in front of others. They've felt much more confident . . . I think they feel that there's space in the lesson . . . I've got plenty of time to go round, I don't have to worry mainly about the discipline, there'll be no boys lurking around the classroom or anything.'*

A colleague who taught an all boys' group provided an interesting contrast!

> *'Whatever you do, it has to be a game and it has to involve people getting knocked over . . . I mean noughts and crosses – anything- there's got to be a sort of element of violence to it.'*

However, teachers reported that the boys had worked harder in single sex groups, as they had had fewer distractions and there had been 'less playing to the gallery.' This teacher had taught some of the boys in a mixed situation for their second language (Spanish) and commented on the contrast.

Changing groupings within a mixed class

Some schools may not wish to, or may be unable to group pupils according to gender. They can nonetheless experiment with different groupings within a mixed class in an attempt to maximise the learning opportunities for both boys and girls. Opportunities can be offered for pupils to work in single sex groups, mixed groups or friendship groups. Some pupils articulated support for the notion of teacher intervention to formulate groups. When given a free choice, they 'played safe' and worked with friends or pupils from their form. They felt they would not have the confidence to choose to work with pupils from other form groups, whom they did not know, but with whom they were now in a set. They felt, however, that if their teacher were to change groupings frequently, they could benefit from the different perspectives these pupils had to offer

By using different settings, pupils can benefit in a variety of ways:

- by learning to work co-operatively with a range of people instead of simply with close friends;
- by developing new skills;
  - (i) boys are more confident about risk taking than girls;
  - (ii) girls are often better organised;
  - (iii) girls find it easier to work co-operatively in a group situation;
  - (iv) girls tend to discuss ideas and negotiate. A boy will be exposed to more language when working in a mixed group, than when working with another boy.

'Boys will be boys': the pressure of masculinity

As discussed in Chapter 1 (page 8) there appears to be more pressure on boys to conform to socially accepted gender norms. Some boys feel the need to live up to a 'macho' image which defines their behaviour in class and limits the activities in which they will voluntarily engage. In certain areas of the curriculum such as English and modern languages, the curriculum can be alienating, because it is personalised and requires pupils to reveal things about themselves and their feelings. To avoid embarrassment and, because they feel it is inappropriate for boys to admit to, let alone discuss feelings, many boys choose either to remain silent or to disrupt the classroom discussion. By contrast, this type of work favours girls, firstly because discussions of personal matters are often enacted amongst women in their family life, and secondly since it is seen to be gender-appropriate for girls. Indeed, from a very young age, girls can be seen to congregate in groups at break and lunch times and to be engaged in talking and discussing, whereas many boys are involved in physical exercise such as football which precludes talk of an intimate nature.

Boys' preferred learning styles

Teachers have often attempted to engage boys by tuning in to their preferred learning styles. Many boys, it would seem -

- enjoy the competitive edge offered by games;
- prefer instant feedback (tests marked on the spot);
- like to be engaged actively;
- are motivated by IT;
- dislike reading and writing.

It is important to note these preferences but, at the same time, to avoid falling into the trap of promoting stereotypical 'macho' images, which would be antipathetical not only to girls, but also to some of the boys.

Boys and computer games

Similarly, computer games seem to appeal to boys more than girls possibly because of the competitive slant and their link with sport (improve your score). Equally, many girls may be put off by the violent nature of some of these games. Whilst many may have thought that these types of games offered a welcome populist introduction to ICT, it is debatable if any direct benefit (apart possibly from a certain degree of manual dexterity and speed of reactions) can be gained from the disproportionate amount of time some boys spend with these sorts of games. Certainly, they are detrimental to language development as they are played in isolation and no literacy skills are required. While boys are seeking to improve on their last score, girls are more likely to be reading or interacting in small groups, thus enhancing their already superior skills in the language curriculum.

Oracy in the English curriculum

Researchers in the English curriculum have sought to make personal discussions more open to boys by giving them roles to play. This enables them to take part in discussions, but at the same time preserve their distance. This is a technique which can very easily be employed in the modern languages curriculum, where instead of talking about their home life, hobbies or families, pupils could be given a card with various details, from which to construct themselves a fictitious and therefore non-self revelatory identity.

'Real boys don't read books': thinking about reading

Some would argue that reading is in decline in our schools. Reading is 'everywhere and nowhere'. People assume that pupils engage in reading regularly during the school day. However, it may be increasingly true that pupils rarely read chunks of continuous text and very infrequently read for longer than five minutes either at school or at home.

Reading is an area of the school curriculum which has been shown to be gendered. Indeed, reading has grown to be construed more as a girls' appropriate task than a boys' task. This may be due, in part, to the fact that in many families literacy is considered to be the responsibility of mothers, as it draws on skills which women possess. Thus for working class boys, working on literacy skills runs contrary to the behaviour expected within their white working class culture. Within this culture, reading and writing are deemed 'girlish' or effeminate. This is precisely the sort of label these white working class boys want to avoid at all costs.

Literacy researchers have made distinctions between girls' and boys' attitudes towards reading, suggesting that girls are more likely to 'read for pleasure' whereas boys associate reading purely with schoolwork and do not choose to read anything other than what they are forced to read. It is crucial therefore, if we want boys to read more often and more willingly, that we consider the nature of the reading material and the form in which it is presented. In terms of genre, the HMI report *'Boys and English'* (1993) found that there were marked differences in reading tastes between boys and girls. Boys' preferred topics include horror, science-fiction, fantasy, adventure, football, fishing and computers. Boys seem more ready to read comics and magazines than books, and may have a preference for non-fiction over fiction. Further, the impact of IT which has acquired a positive image for many boys, can be exploited in this area. Boys appear to be much more enthusiastic about reading on-line or from CD-ROMS than from the written page.

Reading and MFL

The importance of reading in the modern languages classroom has diminished considerably over the last decade. There has been a volte-face from the days when new language was introduced in a text and then worked on in a series of (most often written) exercises. In some modern National Curriculum coursebooks, one finds it difficult to locate longer texts and the incidence of 'reading for pleasure' in a foreign language, although explicitly mentioned in the National Curriculum Levels of Attainment, is frequently side-lined. Many, myself included, would argue that we do this at our peril, since the written word presents us with a visual model of the language. Whilst it is inarguably the case that pupils are exposed to much more language in an oral and aural sense than in more traditional courses, it is important to acknowledge that pupils' preferred learning styles differ, and for some this visual picture can be a useful aid to memory. Moreover, it seems likely that there is a strong correlation between the amount of reading pupils engage in and the quality of their writing.

It is worthwhile devoting a departmental meeting to reviewing the resources available for reading for pleasure, with a view to updating them to provide a range of attractive and accessible readers (within the obvious constraints imposed on departments by increasingly limited capitation). As is the case for listening, it is important to motivate pupils in the early stages of language learning by providing material which is readily comprehensible, so that they can gain confidence in their ability to read in a foreign language by experiencing success. The confidence gained should then serve them well as they tackle longer and more complex texts.

Auditing available reading material

- Which age group is this text intended for?
- Which age group would it appeal to?
- Does the text look attractive/interesting/accessible/dull/difficult/uninspiring? *(look at the cover and the text inside).*
- How readable is the text? How much text is there on a page? Is there any pictorial support? Are the sentences / vocabulary / syntax simple or complex?
- Is there a word list provided at the back of the book?
- Are there any activities to form a focus for the reading? Are these straight forward 'fun' activities which can be completed quickly and with relative ease or are they more like higher level GCSE questions?

Cataloguing available resources

This may not take long! In order to spot obvious gaps in terms of types of book, it can be a useful exercise to list readers for each Key Stage according to genre (see Appendix 5 for a possible pro forma). This information could be used as compelling evidence of the need for additional resources. Some schools have been able to use monies made available for the School Library to purchase foreign language readers. Indeed, some schools have chosen to allocate each of their teaching groups half an hour per fortnight in the library specifically for reading for pleasure. Others have organised a carousel of activities over a standard double lesson, whereby students work in the library and are engaged in reading for pleasure, dictionary work, CD-Rom based tasks and information gathering about a country using available reference materials (in response to a 'quiz').

WRITING

Girls seem to enjoy writing more than boys and often receive higher marks for their writing than boys. Girls' presentation is invariably much neater and they are generally able to write at greater length. Statistics show that girls outperform boys in National Curriculum English at seven, eleven and fourteen and that the gap widens with age (*Excellence in schools*, 1997). It could be that writing has come to be construed as a girls' role in the same way as reading is seen as 'girlish'. Many girls enjoy writing outside school, whereas a fair proportion of boys do no writing at all outside the classroom.

Where pupils are given the option of 'free writing' within the English curriculum, the themes chosen are often diametrically opposed and conform largely to gender-stereotypes. Thus girls are typically more likely to write about horses, and boys to choose to write about crashes, war or murder. The gendered nature of society tends to be very pervasive and very rigid.

As far as modern languages are concerned, much of the writing may again be alienating for the boys. Much of the letter writing/penfriend scenarios are more likely to appeal to girls and the ways in which they have been socialised. Wherever possible, it is important to offer alternatives which will be more motivating for boys. Instead of writing a penfriend letter about your home, pupils could opt to produce an estate agent's leaflet on their home, or a 'dream-home', or indeed a humorous 'hard sell' of a garden shed. It is worth looking for other options which should appeal equally to both sexes and which allow for an element of personalisation and creativity, such as an alternative school prospectus, a tourist leaflet for the local area, hotel brochures, a magazine style description of the autumn 'look' with photographs or drawings. Such work lends itself to the use of IT and ultimately to display.

Pupils could be encouraged to write collaboratively in pairs or small groups (teachers could allow a free choice of groupings or arrange for mixed sex groupings). Pupils have suggested that they enjoy working together on a writing project as they do not experience the 'isolation of the lone writer', it then becomes less daunting, and the responsibility for the mistakes is shared. Inevitably also, such an approach to writing involves a certain degree of peer learning, which is seen by pupils as positive. Joint responsibility for a piece of writing may indeed encourage more thorough checking than an individual piece of work written in an exercise book. As the writing is a joint venture, it seems reasonable to expect a longer piece of work.

Where free writing is an option, greater care needs to be exercised in the choice of topics to offer a range which can appeal to a cross-section of pupil interests. If a piece of narrative is required, the experience of the English curriculum suggests that boys can be helped to write at greater length by providing a framework of ideas and sub-headings instead of simply a title, which can be seen as very daunting. This can be done at different levels according to the ability of the individuals. See ***A*** for a simple 'jigsaw' narrative, which provides a clear framework, but which allows for a degree of personalisation. Example ***B*** is more demanding as there are a number of grammatical pitfalls. Cloze activities of this nature can be very prescriptive and do not allow for much creativity. Pupils would find it helpful to look at the text together, with possible suggestions listed on the board or on the OHP. The obvious danger of mixing the auxiliaries in the Perfect Tense could be avoided in this way by listing potential activities in two columns (*avoir* and *être*). The notion of whole class brainstorming of ideas prior to individual writing can help to support all pupils' writing. Thus a piece of writing, based on the theme of a disastrous day, could begin with a teacher providing and practising possible phrases such as 'I knocked over . . . ', 'I dropped . . . ', 'I broke a . . . ', 'I burnt . . . ', 'I lost . . . ', 'I forgot . . . ' followed by some personal accident phrases – "I twisted/sprained/broke/fell (downstairs, in a river, over the dog etc.) These expressions can be left either on the board or on the OHP and pupils can be encouraged to select from them, edit and amend them as they wish to formulate their own versions.

A Jigsaw narrative:

Ich bin (***wann?**wie?**mit wem?***) in die Stadt gefahren. Ich habe (***was?***) gekauft.

Wann?	Letzten Samstag / gestern / am Wochenende / gestern abend
Wie?	Mit dem Bus / mit dem Zug / mit dem Auto / mit dem Fahrrad / mit dem Motorrad
Mit wem?	Mit meiner Freundin / mit meiner Schwester / mit meiner Mutter
	Mit meinem Freund / mit meinem Bruder / mit meinem Vater
Was?	Eine Jeans / ein Geschenk / einen Pulli / eine Zeitschrift / Schokolade / Tennisschuhe / eine CD

B. Framework for a narrative: Une visite

Le voyage en .... a duré .... heures. Je suis donc arrivé(e) vers .... heures. Tout d'abord j'ai .... Ensuite je suis .... C'était vraiment .... L'après-midi .... et .... Le soir, vu qu'il pleuvait on a décidé de .... Le lendemain, il faisait encore beau donc nous sommes allé(e)s voir .... C'était ....

Supporting writing through Information and Communications Technology (ICT)

Boys' written work is stereotypically considered rushed and scruffy. ICT has been shown to play an important role in motivating pupils and particularly boys to write (see T. Atkinson's book *'Hands off! It's my go'*, for a more detailed discussion of the benefits of ICT). Pupils feel pleased with the image of their text on the screen and with the end-product. Word-processing makes error-correction non-threatening and less laborious. Interestingly, pupils often seem to take more care over their spelling when word-processing than when writing by hand, taking the time to stop and look words up and co-operating with a partner to check work more thoroughly than is usually the case. Researchers have found that pupils are willing to write up to 50% more when word-processing than when writing by hand.

Girls and ICT

Girls have been shown to be less confident in their own ability with ICT and often less positive about the use of ICT. This may be in part due to the fact that in many schools ICT still retains some of the 'male' image associated with Computer Science. Computer rooms are often seen as 'male territory'. Consequently, in schools where optional lunch-time computer clubs are on offer, only a small minority of girls attend regularly. Research has shown that girls have less access to the machines and less assistance from their teachers, since boys tend to dominate both the machines and the teacher time. This is a matter of concern for teachers given the importance attributed to the new technologies and the implications for future employment. It is essential that issues of continuing disadvantage and inequality for girls are not lost amidst the growing concern for under-achieving boys. (See C. Opie (1998) 'Whose turn next? Gender issues in information technology' in A. Clark and E. Millard (eds.) *Gender in the secondary curriculum*, for a more detailed discussion of this).

Mentoring

Mentoring is a strategy which has been employed by a number of schools in an attempt to improve performance. Often, such a strategy focuses on pupils on the D/C border at GCSE, as these statistics are so important for the league tables, and this is where teachers feel they can make the difference. If this strategy can be shown to be effective, it is worth considering how it can be made manageable across all pupils rather than favouring the few.

Points for departmental discussion

- What impact do our arrangements for grouping have on pupils?
- What alternatives could we consider?
- Can we do anything to ensure that boys and girls get a fair share of the teacher's attention?
- Can we improve our stock of reading material to appeal to a wider range of interest? Can we include some non-fiction?
- Can we build into our schemes of work a regular reading for pleasure slot (maybe once a fortnight?) and provide a system for recording what pupils are reading?
- Can we look at alternative approaches to writing that are more 'boy friendly'?
- Can we build in opportunities for paired creative writing?

- Can we integrate ICT into our schemes of work more readily to benefit from the increased motivation word-processing brings to writing, particularly among boys? At the same time, can we ensure that girls have time and support to develop their skills in ICT?

FURTHER READING

'Can boys do better?', R.Bray, P.Downes, C. Gardner, G.Hannan, N. Parsons, MAPS (SHA) Ltd., 1997, Bristol

'Improving boys' literacy', G. Frater, The Basic Skills Agency, London, 1997 (www.basic-skills.co.uk)

'Raising boys' achievement', Kirklees Education Advisory Service, 1996

'Differently Literate. Boys, girls and the schooling of literacy', E. Millard, 1996, Falmer Press, London

'Raising boys' achievement', J. Pickering, 1997, Network Educational Press Ltd., Stafford

Further thoughts

There seems to be growing evidence of male disaffection with schooling in general. One of the challenges for the next decade is how to address this anti-learning culture which can have such a prejudicial effect on the learning of both boys and girls. A whole school strategy is needed to address these issues, although attempts to change these attitudes will need more wide-ranging support. Awareness needs to be raised among staff, pupils and parents of the dramatic differences in achievement between boys and girls. Boys need to be encouraged to re-assess their view on the importance of school. The PSE curriculum may provide an arena in which boys can be challenged to look at the hard reality of exam results and explore the underlying causes. Equally, girls could be encouraged to challenge the boys' domination of the classroom by developing assertiveness skills, to have more self-confidence and to consider a future not simply in line with traditional career paths, which may not enable them to fulfil their potential. Within schools, the use of staff and pupil mentors has been shown to make a difference, by raising the profile of school work. The involvement and education of parents/guardians as partners in this process is also essential, but this is not an easy task. Schools need to be able to promote an atmosphere of 'it's cool to work hard at school' rather than the converse.

If we are to bring about any fundamental change in girls' and boys' performance and attitudes in modern languages, the relative status and position of the subject in school needs to be re-assessed probably as part of the language curriculum as a whole. Ideally, one might hope for a whole school approach towards language and literacy which would not accept that boys' writing is inevitably 'scruffy' and rushed or that girls are 'naturally' good at language. It clearly has not been enough simply to make the study of a modern foreign language core to the age of sixteen. Some would argue strongly for the introduction of modern languages in the primary sector, whilst others would argue for a foreign language for all to the age of eighteen (Hawkins, 1996). It is indeed only by changing expectations and the status of modern languages in schools that teachers can start to make a difference.

At times the messages we try to convey are at odds with the images in the popular press and the media. It would be helpful to have strong role models in the public domain – in politics, in sport and in business, who speak a foreign language competently instead of reinforcing the belief that 'everyone speaks English'. Nearer to home, teachers of modern languages need to reflect on the curriculum that is on offer and the learning styles most frequently used to access that curriculum, to test whether both serve too often to alienate many pupils across the many divides in school (gender, ability, social background). Furthermore, it is alarming to note the steadily falling numbers of students studying modern languages to 'A' Level, and if we are not to be defeatist, we need to consider the underlying causes of this worrying trend and take action to improve attitudes lower down the school.

This text has outlined a range of practical strategies for improving the delivery of modern languages in school. A key issue is to examine ways of translating the curriculum into more meaningful contexts for young people, their interests and aspirations. At the same time, teachers need to show empathy for the difficulties pupils experience in learning a foreign language, remembering Eric Hawkins' useful metaphor of 'gardening in a gale'. It is important not to overface and thus demotivate pupils by demonstrating what they do not know and cannot do and, wherever possible, to plan for recapitulation, to help them to commit key vocabulary and structure to memory and to render this process less tedious by using a variety of media. The importance of bringing the study of a foreign language to life by links with the foreign country cannot be over-emphasised. These links can take the form of educational visits or be classroom-based, taking advantage of new technology to communicate directly with learners in other institutions, or the use of video footage can offer an insight into life in the foreign country.

Finally of course, against the current backdrop of raising achievement, any compensatory action should not be limited to specific pupils, whether it be those on the D/C border, boys or girls. There seems to be an inherent danger in the current focus on boys' under-achievement that issues which continue to affect girls in and beyond school will be side-lined. Notwithstanding the pressures on teachers to raise attainment, the over-arching principle of schooling should be to aim to equalise opportunities so that boys and girls are not limited and bound by their gender but can achieve their full potential.

Bibliography

Askew, S. & Ross, C. (1988) Boys don't cry, Open University Press, Milton Keynes

Atkinson, T. (1992) Hands off! It's my go. IT in the languages classroom, CILT, NCET, London, Coventry

Bray, R., Downes, P., Gardner, C., Hannan, G., Parsons, N. (1997) Can boys do better?, Secondary Heads Association, Bristol

Clark, A. & Trafford, A.J. (1994) A study of the effect of gender on pupil attitudes and performance, University of Sheffield

Clark, A. & Trafford, A.J. (1995) Boys into Modern Languages: an investigation of the discrepancy in attitudes and performance between boys and girls in modern languages, in Gender and Education, Vol. 7, No. 3.

DfEE (1990, 1994, 1996, 1997) Statistical Bulletin, HMSO, London

DfEE (1997) Excellence in Schools, HMSO, London

Delamont, S. (1990, 2nd edition) Sex roles and the school, Routledge, London

Dickson, P. (1996) Using the Target Language, NFER, Slough

Harris, S., Nixon, J., & Rudduck, J. (1993) School Work, Homework and Gender, in Gender and Education, Vol.5, No. 1,

Harris, V. (1992) Fair enough? Equal opportunities and modern languages, CILT, London

Harris, V. (1997) Teaching learners how to learn: strategy training in the ML classroom, CILT, London

Hawkins, E. ed. (1996) 30 Years of language teaching, CILT, London

HMI (1985) Boys and modern languages, DES, London

Kelly, A. (1987) The construction of masculine science in Arnot, M. & Weiner, G.(eds.) *Gender and the politics of schooling*, Open University Press, Milton Keynes

Kruse, A. (1996) Single-sex settings: Pedagogies for girls and boys in Danish schools, in P.F.Muphy and C.V.Gipps 'Equity in the classroom', The Falmer Press, London

MacDonald, M. Schooling and the reproduction of class and gender relations in Barton, L., Meigham, R. & Walker, S. *Schooling, Ideology and the Curriculum*, Falmer Press, Lewes (1980)

Mahoney, P. (1985) Schools for the boys, Hutchinson, London

Moys, A. (1997) The challenges of secondary education in E. Hawkins (ed.) 30 Years of Language Teaching, CILT, London

OFSTED (1993) Boys and English, HMSO, London

OFSTED (1994) Modern Foreign Languages KS3 First Year 1992–93, HMSO, London

OFSTED / E.O.C. (1997) The gender divide: performance differences between boys and girls at school, HMSO, London

Opie, C. (1998) Whose turn next? Gender issues in Information Technology, in A. Clark and E.Millard (eds.) Gender in the secondary curriculum: Balancing the books, Routledge, London

Powell, R (1986) Boys, girls and languages in school, CILT, London

Scott, M. (1980) 'Teach her a lesson; sexist curriculum in patriarchal education' in D. Spender and E. Sarah (eds.) *Learning to lose: Sexism and Education*, The Women's press, London, pp97–120

Spender, D. (1992) 2nd edition. Invisible Women. The Schooling Scandal, The Women's Press, London

Smithers, A. & Robinson, P. (1995) Co-Educational and single sex schooling, University of Manchester (available through the Headmasters Conference)

Stanworth, M. (1983) Gender and schooling: a study of sexual division in the classroom, Hutchinson, London

Warnock, M. (1991), article in Times Educational Supplement, London

Appendices

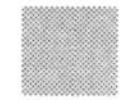

Appendix 1a

Interview Schedule (Pupils)

1. Which foreign languages (FL) do you study? How long have you been studying them?

2. If you were to rank all your subjects in order of importance, where would you place FL? Can you explain your answer?

3. Where would FL rank in terms of difficulty?

4. What makes FL different or more difficult than other subjects?

5. What do you enjoy most about FL? Why?

6. What do you enjoy least about FL? Why?

7. How much homework do you get in FL? Is that more or less than in other subjects?

8. How could FL be made more interesting or more enjoyable?

9. What effect does the teacher have on your attitudes to FL?

(Does it matter whether your teacher is male or female? What are the qualities of a good FL teacher in your view?)

Appendix 1b

Interview Schedule (Staff)

1. How do pupils perceive FL?

2. What do they particularly enjoy?

3. What do they dislike?

4. Do you perceive any gender difference in pupils in terms of:

    - attitudes towards FL

    - Approach to classwork in FL

- approach to homework in FL
- achievement in FL

Do you have any views on why there are differences?

Do you think boys and girls respond differently to different styles of teaching/learning?

Which teaching/learning styles have you found to motivate boys / girls?

5. How are pupils grouped for teaching? Where there is setting, is there an even distribution of boys and girls in all sets?

6. What could be done to motivate boys in FL?

APPENDIX 2

GENDER AND MODERN LANGUAGES: PUPIL QUESTIONNAIRE

This questionnaire aims to discover pupils' attitudes towards language learning at school and to find out how language learning could be made more enjoyable.

BACKGROUND INFORMATION

Sex Male ☐ Female ☐

Type of School 11–16 mixed comprehensive ☐ 11–18 mixed comprehensive ☐

BACKGROUND TO LANGUAGES LEARNING

1. Please indicate the number of years you have studied languages

   French . . . . . . years German . . . . . . years Spanish . . . . . . years

   Russian . . . . . . years Other (________________) . . . . . . years

2. Which languages are you studying for GCSE?

3. Have you ever been on a school trip or exchange with the languages department?

   No ☐ Yes ☐ *(please give details – country, length of stay, value in learning the language)*

4. Does your school have an exchange link? Yes ☐ No ☐

5. Does the department run other trips to France/Germany/Spain? Yes ☐ No ☐

6. Is your current teacher – Male ☐ Female ☐ ?

7. Over the last five years what has been the sex of your languages teachers?

Always female	☐	Always male	☐
4 female, 1 male	☐	3 female, 2 male	☐
2 female, 3 male	☐	1 female, 4 male	☐

8. Do you intend to continue with the study of a foreign language beyond GCSE?

Yes ☐ No ☐

9. How much homework do you get per week on average?

0–1 hour ☐ 1–2 hour ☐ more than 2 hours ☐

10. What sort of homework do you get? (*Please mark the boxes using the key below*)

1 = every lesson **2 = once a week** **3 = once a fortnight**
4 = rarely **5 = never**

Vocabulary learning	☐	Reading comprehension	☐
Exercise from a book	☐	Writing letters/accounts	☐
Other (*Please specify*)	☐	....	

Importance of foreign languages (*please number the subjects below in order of importance; 1 = the most important subject in your view, 10 = the least important*)

English	....	Matehmatics	....
Science	....	French/German/Spanish	....
History	....	Geography	....
Technology	....	RE	....
PE/Games	....	Art	....

Difficulty of foreign languages (*please number the subjects below in order of difficulty 1 = the most difficult subject in your view, 10 = the easiest/least difficult*)

English	....	Matehmatics	....
Science	....	French/German/Spanish	....
History	....	Geography	....
Technology	....	RE	....
PE/Games	....	Art	....

Language Learning

1. Do you have regular access to – (*Please number the boxes using the key below*)

TV & video ☐ Tape recorders ☐ OHP ☐

Satellite TV ☐ Information Technology ☐

Coursebooks for GCSE ☐ Foreign Language assistants ☐

1 = every lesson **2 = once a week** **3 = once a fortnight**
4 = rarely **5 = never**

2. How often do you do the following activities? (*Please number the boxes using the key above*)

Listening to a tape	☐	Reading comprehension	☐
Exercise from a book	☐	Grammar	☐
Copying from the board/book	☐	Extended writing	☐
Teacher/whole class oral work	☐	Pair work	☐
Group work	☐	Watching a video	☐
Using IT	☐	Independent learning	☐
Reading for pleasure	☐	Games	☐

Other ☐ (*Please specify*)..

3. Which of the following activities do you find most useful? (*Please number 1 = most useful, 14 = least useful or mark with a X if you do not do this type of work in your lessons*)

Listening to a tape	☐	Reading comprehension	☐
Exercise from a book	☐	Grammar	☐
Copying from the board/book	☐	Extended writing	☐
Teacher/whole class oral work	☐	Pair work	☐
Group work	☐	Watching a video	☐
Using IT	☐	Independent learning	☐
Reading for pleasure	☐	Games	☐

4. Which of the following activities do you find most enjoyable? (*Please number 1 = most enjoyable, 14 = least enjoyable or mark with a X if you do not do this type of work in your lessons*)

Listening to a tape	☐	Reading comprehension	☐
Exercise from a book	☐	Grammar	☐
Copying from the board/book	☐	Extended writing	☐
Teacher/whole class oral work	☐	Pair work	☐
Group work	☐	Watching a video	☐
Using IT	☐	Independent learning	☐
Reading for pleasure	☐	Games	☐

5. What could be done to increase the motivation of Year 11 pupils in modern languages in your opinion?

....

....

6. What are the qualities of a good language teacher in your view?

....

....

Thank you for taking the time to complete this questionnaire, Ann Clark, University of Sheffield

APPENDIX 3

PROGRESS REVIEW

Year ... Progress Review

.... Term 199__ Language ....

Name .... Form .... Teacher ....

1. Which aspects of your studies have given you most satisfaction this term?

2. How would you describe your progress this term in each of the four main skill areas?

	Pleasing	**Satisfactory**	**Unsatisfactory**	**Poor**
Listening				
Speaking				
Reading				
Writing				

3. Which areas of your studies have you been least happy with and why?

....

4. How would you rate your level of application this term on the following scale?

	Maximum Effort		**Coasting**		**Lazy**
In class	1	2	3	4	5
At home	1	2	3	4	5

5. Have you learnt vocabulary .... ?

A. regularly and conscientiously B. reasonably well
C. occasionally D. hardly ever properly

6. Do you present your work .... ?

A. neatly and with pride B. reasonably neatly
C. legibly D. sloppily

7. In which areas do you need to improve over the next term?

....

8. What will you do of a practical nature to help you achieve this?

....

....

Signed .... Date of Completion ....

Source: The Ecclesbourne School, Duffield.

Appendix 4

Agree/Disagree

		✔		
		Agree	?	Disagree
1.	The nature of the language curriculum can be off-putting because it is so mundane and trivialising or it is personal and self-reveatory			
2.	Boys show less urgency generally about their studies and concern for their progress			
3.	Boys monopolise teacher attention			
4.	Teachers fire more questions at boys in the whole group oral work			
5.	Boys prefer oral and aural work to writing activities			
6.	Boys prefer greater choice of activity and resent working tightly to highly prescriptive arrangements			
7.	Boys are less reliable about homeworks			
8.	Girls take more care over their work than boys			
9.	Boys take less care about handwriting and presentation generally than girls			
10.	It is easy to be beguiled by good presentation into thinking that written work is better than it really is			
11.	Subject matter is more frequently geared to girls' interests			
12.	The introduction of premature setting arrangements guarantees a predominance of boys in 'lower ability' groups			

Appendix 5

Catalogue of Readers for KS3

Science fiction	Horror	Adventure	Crime	Non-fiction

Cartoons	Humour	Sport	Hobbies	Young people	Animals